ALL COLOR BOOK OF
EGYPTIAN MYTHOLOGY
BY RICHARD PATRICK
INTRODUCTION BY MARGARET DROWER

CHARTWELL
BOOKS, INC.

First published in Great Britain in 1972 by
Octopus Books Ltd
This 1989 edition
published by
Chartwell Books, Inc.
A Division of Book Sales Inc.
110 Enterprise Avenue
Secaucus
New Jersey 07094

© 1974 Octopus Books Ltd

ISBN 1-55521-358-8

Produced by Mandarin Offset
Printed in Hong Kong

CONTENTS

INTRODUCTION

The history of ancient Egyptian civilization falls, by the convention of modern historians, into three main periods or phases: the Old Kingdom, or Pyramid Age; the Middle Kingdom, sometimes misleadingly called the Feudal Age; and the New Kingdom, when Egypt became an imperial power and reached the apex of her prosperity and influence. These 'Kingdoms', however, are no more than landmarks or peak periods in what was in reality a continuous process of political and cultural development lasting through almost three thousand years of pharanoic rule. The roots of Egyptian civilization lay deep in her past, before written records began and before the country became a single kingdom united under one rule. They can be dimly glimpsed in the simple material remains of the prehistoric period – the designs on pots found in the graves, the decoration on stone palettes for grinding eyepaint or on ivory combs and knife-handles. Memories of an earlier age also survive in religious literature, in the very ancient texts inscribed in some of the Old Kingdom pyramids, and in ritual practices and the insignia and paraphernalia of royal and temple panoply. Most important of all was the continuing dual nature of Egyptian kingship.

Symmetry and balance were characteristic both of the art and the literature of ancient Egypt, and many heraldic groups of opposing figures symbolized North and South, East and West, Good and Evil, the cultivated land and the desert, Egypt and non-Egypt (i.e. the rest of mankind). In the legends, Truth did battle with Falsehood, Horus the god of fertile Egypt with Seth, the red god of deserts. Above all, Egypt itself was a double kingdom; its pharaoh was 'Lord of the Two Lands', and 'King of Upper and Lower Egypt.' The south, or Upper Egypt, was the narrow strip of cultivated earth on either side of the Nile, sometimes only a few miles wide, which stretched from the cataract at Aswan to the ancient capital Memphis, near modern Cairo. Lower Egypt was the wide alluvial Delta, its waterways spreading fanlike from the apex near Memphis and Heliopolis towards the two hundred mile long coastline of the Mediterranean. In popular memory these Two Lands were once separate, but had been united by a certain Menes, who was thought to have been the first king of the First Dynasty. Thenceforward the memory of the unification was preserved in the titles and insignia of the King and some officials. The king wore a double crown, the Red Crown of the Delta being combined with the white mitre of Upper Egypt; on his throne the heraldic plants symbolic of North and South were entwined, and on his forehead he sometimes wore twin diadems, the symbols of the vulture-goddess Nekhebet of Upper

Egypt and the cobra-goddess Buto of the Delta. The king's coronation rites were performed in duplicate, once for the north, and once for the south. By temperament and in their way of life the dwellers of Upper Egypt were different from those of the Delta, and they spoke a different dialect as they do to this day. Their cult practices and beliefs were therefore very different and many of their myths had a strongly local flavour.

Modern archaeological discovery in the various countries of the Levant has given the lie to the old belief that the valley of the Nile was the cradle of civilization, and that everything began in Egypt. We know nowadays that most of the important discoveries which were landmarks in the early progress of mankind occurred elsewhere, in the hills of Palestine and Syria, the alluvial plain of Mesopotamia or the uplands of Persia and Anatolia, and sometimes even further afield. Thus the Egyptians were not, so far as we can see, the first agriculturalists, nor were they the first potters, nor the first workers in metal. Moreover the idea of writing – that essential invention without which man cannot convey his ideas and develop an urban society – probably reached Egypt from some neighbouring country. Nevertheless, the brilliant use to which the Egyptians put these newly-learned skills soon placed them in the forefront of ancient civilizations. Because of their relative isolation, and the unique nature of their way of life, Egyptian civilization developed a highly individual character which was the wonder and admiration of most of their neighbours.

The Greeks recognized the uniqueness of Egypt. The historian Herodotus, who visited the Nile valley in the fifth century BC, was filled with astonishment with what he saw and wrote as follows: – 'Just as the Egyptians have a climate peculiar to themselves, and their river is different in its nature from all other rivers, so they have made themselves customs and laws of a kind contrary to those of all other men.' Of the native customs he describes, none were more strange in his eyes or more different from Greek religious practice than the cults of the various gods and goddesses and their animal counterparts. These rites and beliefs he found everywhere, and concluded that the Egyptians 'were beyond measure religious, more than any other nation'.

It is probably true to say that among no other ancient people were the strands of belief in the supernatural so closely interwoven with their daily lives, their personal relationships, their hopes and fears, and their attitude to authority. The day-to-day hazards of existence were the work of hostile powers; scorpions and snakes could be warded off by amulets worn on the body, or incantations written on scrolls and kept in the house. In times of hazard such as childbirth and illness the deities of the hearth and home were invoked, and Bes, the domestic god who watched over sleep, was carved on the bed and walls. Sowing and harvest were times when offerings must be made to the gods

who gave success to these operations, and the River Nile, itself a god, must be placated lest he rise too swiftly or be too niggardly with his life-giving waters.

Besides these potentially hostile or friendly spirits of the house and field and threshing-floor, there were greater deities who represented the various forces of nature. In the early days, local tribal gods in the various regions of the country had been embodiments of different aspects of nature. Then some villages grew into towns or cities, while others became grouped into districts, and districts into political units (for administrative purposes, the so called 'nomes'), and the city- or nome-gods grew in importance until some were so widely worshipped that they became national gods. Thus the growth of the pantheon reflects the political growth of Egypt from its tribal origins in predynastic times. Similarly the introduction into the pantheon of newcomers reflects the influx of foreigners or of foreign influences either at times of weakness when the country was subject to immigration, or in times of strength when she controlled an empire abroad.

In the Old Kingdom, about 2600 BC, early Egyptian civilization reached a very high level. The whole country was efficiently organized under the centralized control of the royal family and power and wealth were concentrated at court. Craftsmen and architects, quarrymen and masons worked for the king and the small circle of officials surrounding him, many of whom were royal princes. Temples were erected to the great gods; Ptah the god of the capital, Memphis, Ra the god of Heliopolis from whom the king claimed descent, Hathor the great goddess of Dendera, and Horus whose incarnation the king was thought to be. However the resources of the country, in manpower and materials, were lavished in greatest measure on the building of huge pyramid tombs for the kings themselves, on costly burial places for their relatives and dependents, and on the endowment of priesthoods which were to carry on for ever the funerary cult of the dead. All these were non-productive ends which dissipated the country's wealth. Bankruptcy, the breakdown of central control and the dissipation of power into the hands of the nobles led to anarchy and civil war and for a time disrupted the realm. Asiatic Bedouin, in the confusion, poured into the Delta, while tribesmen from Nubia overran Upper Egypt, and art declined and trade dwindled.

Shortly before 2000 BC, the country was reunited by a Theban family of warrior-kings, whose energy and competence restored order and inaugurated the Middle Kingdom (about 2050-1780 BC). The Thebans had started their career as nomarchs (that is, rulers of their local nome), and they had gained the ascendancy with the help of other nomarchs almost equally powerful. These nobles continued to wield considerable influence under

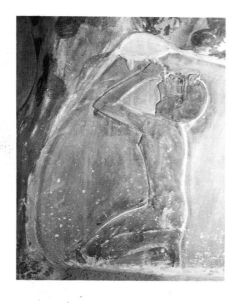

the crown, and lived in their own domains in almost royal style; their palaces were miniature courts, they could command the work of craftsmen and artists, and some of the finest works of art of the Middle Kingdom came not from the capital, but from the nomes. Cults of local gods such as Sobek of the Faiyum, Min of Coptos and Amon of Thebes flourished.

The Middle Kingdom was followed by a second period of weakness and confusion from which few material remains have survived. Foreigners from nearby Palestine poured into the Delta and for a time controlled virtually the whole country; they were finally expelled, after bitter conflict, by another Theban family whose triumph ushered in the most glorious era of Egypt's history, the New Kingdom (*circa* 1570–1085 BC). Now the armies of Pharaoh, experienced in warfare, set about the conquest of Palestine. Fortresses secured the eastern and western borders of the Delta against possible attack, and then the Egyptians marched north till they reached the River Euphrates in Syria, not far from the present Turkish border. In the south, the Sudan as far as the fourth cataract was brought under Egyptian control and the gold mines of Nubia were exploited to the full.

Egypt was now the wealthiest country in the world. Corn and cattle, timber and precious metals, incense, wine and oil, the tribute of the empire, poured into her treasuries, and emissaries from distant potentates brought the riches of Mesopotamia, Anatolia and the Aegean as diplomatic gifts. The gods were the chief beneficiaries of this wealth, and especially the King's family god Amon, who as Amon-Ra became the state god. Huge temples were built for him, the elegant temple of Luxor and the large and elaborate temple at Karnak. Added to by successive kings, this great metropolitan shrine received its most imposing addition in the mighty pillared hall built by Seti I about 1310 BC and then was completed by his son Rameses II, sometimes called Rameses the Great. This remarkable man, during his long reign of sixty seven years, carried out a stupendous building programme not only in every cult centre of Egypt but also in Nubia, where he dedicated no less than seven temples to the local gods and the great gods. In these temples he is depicted as a god himself and on the facade of the largest, the rock-temple of Abu Simbel, (now rescued from the rising waters of the High Dam by a spectacular feat of modern engineering), four colossal seated statues of the king, nearly seventy feet high, dwarf even the figures of the gods themselves.

Rameses' battle with the Hittites, which is the theme of the reliefs on several of his temples, was virtually Egypt's last imperial encounter. Seventy years later she had lost virtually all her possessions and was even threatened with invasion; though the danger was averted the New Kingdom declined in prosperity and in authority; the administration became corrupt and civil war weakened the throne. In the so-called Late Period, the rule of successive dynasties of foreigners – Libyans, negroes from the

Sudan, Assyrians and finally Persians left Egypt totally bereft of inspiration and struggling vainly against crippling taxation and military occupation.

Persian rule in Egypt ended in 332 BC with the arrival of the Macedonian, Alexander the Great. Though he stayed only a short time in Egypt, he was welcomed as a deliverer and paid homage to the gods. After his death the country was organized as a province of the empire and one of Alexander's generals, Ptolemy, was put in charge. Finally in 305 BC he was crowned king of Egypt, as Ptolemy the Saviour. He was the first of a long dynasty of Ptolemies, the last of whom was the son of Cleopatra. Under the Ptolemaic dynasty large numbers of Greek settlers made the country their home and Greek towns sprang up. The greatest of these was Alexandria, founded by Alexander himself on the Mediterranean coast, which rapidly became the greatest city in the Hellenistic world. But although Egypt was now run by foreigners, and Greek was the official language, the native population were allowed to keep their ancient customs and to practise their religion, and the Ptolemies were careful to pay court to the ancient gods, adopting the titles and insignia of Pharaohs, and themselves performing the necessary rites. Much of the information we possess about Egyptian mythology and ritual comes from the huge temples which the Ptolemies built or began to build, and which were completed and further embellished by the Romans who in 30 BC took over the country. The Caesars, like the Ptolemies, are shown on the walls of these temples worshipping the gods of Egypt, but few of them visited the country or knew anything of its traditions. Many Egyptian deities, however, acquired new forms under Hellenistic and Roman rule and the cult of some, such as Isis and Serapis, spread to the farthest ends of the Roman Empire.

Descriptions of life in ancient Egypt have survived in detail and as the climate of Egypt is one of the best in the world, life for all free men was pleasant enough, it would seem. The Egyptian village of the New Kingdom must have been very like the villages of today. Houses were built of unbaked brick, as they are still, and had usually several rooms and steps up to the flat roof on which, in the heat of summer, the family could sleep. Houses of the well-to-do usually had more than one storey and were surrounded by a garden full of palm and acacia trees; in it there was usually a pool on which lotus flowers bloomed and ducks swam. Medium-sized houses had a small walled garden with one or two shady trees and frequently a verandah or porch. Furniture consisted of beds, chairs or stools, and low tables; boxes held clothes, cosmetic articles and other possessions, and wooden stands supported wine jars and large water pots. Mats, woven hangings and flower vases adorned the rooms and the plastered walls were usually painted. The most luxurious houses had a kind of air-conditioning in the form of vents conducting cool air down from the roof and the kitchens and servants' quarters in these luxury villas were often in a separate building.

The Egyptians enjoyed parties and are shown seated at banquets, men and women together, tended by maids who filled the wine bowls and distributed lotus blossoms and perfumed oil to the guests, while musicians played and danced or acrobats tumbled. Pastimes for the wealthy were board games resembling trictrac or ludo, fishing with harpoon or net, and fowling with throwsticks in the marshy papyrus thickets which abounded in wild birds. On hunting expeditions in the desert with their hounds they found ample game, including several species of antelope and gazelle, wild cattle, and that most royal prey, the lion.

Such were the occupations of a busy official during his hours of ease. The peasant or *fellah* had little leisure, if we are to judge by the scenes carved and painted in the tombs of their masters, who are shown inspecting the daily work of their servants and serfs on their estates. Agriculture depended on the river Nile, which flooded its banks with predictable regularity, covering the fields as far as the desert edge. The floodwaters soaked into the earth and when after some weeks they subsided the soil, fertilised by a fresh deposit of silt, was soon dry enough for ploughing. Wheat and barley were the main crops and instead of the cotton of today, flax provided fibres for the manufacture of linen, the universal textile.

Egypt was a totalitarian state; the king's word was the law and legislation was by royal edict. The King was a being apart from all other mortals. His upbringing included instruction in all sports and military accomplishments. By tradition he was braver, wiser and more physically powerful than any of his subjects; none could bend his bow and none shoot so far and so straight. For Pharaoh (the word means 'Great House' and was used in the Late Period to refer, obliquely and respectfully, to the lord of the palace) was a god, a being apart from all mortals; he was deemed to be the child of the sun-god Ra, begotten by Amon-Ra himself who had taken the form of the reigning king at the time of his conception. Khnum the creator-god was thought to have fashioned him in the womb of the queen-mother, and when he was born, the divine child was suckled by wise goddesses. When he succeeded to the throne, he was solemnly crowned by priests dressed as gods, and after thirty years on the throne, further rites revived his waning powers and confirmed his supremacy. The country's well-being depended on him, and it was believed that without his continuing presence, cosmic order would be overthrown, the Nile would cease to flood, and famine and disaster overtake Egypt.

The most admired of professions was that of the scribe. The

tools of their trade were their pencase often inscribed with their name, their ink pot and brushes and their rolls of papyrus. A scribe's apprenticeship was long; he had to learn to draw, in the correct form, some seven hundred hieroglyphic or picture signs and also their hieratic equivalents (the hieroglyphs were carved in stone; hieratic was the simplified form of the signs devised for rapid writing in ink on papyrus or on potsherd or limestone flakes). The word 'hieroglyph' means 'Sacred Writing' and the scribe regarded his calling seriously and before embarking on some new scroll, would pour a libation to Thoth, the god of writing.

Because of its sacred character, the script was conservative. Each pictorial sign was drawn in a way hallowed by custom since its inception and virtually unchanged through three thousand years. Essentially, the system was a simple one. A picture or ideogram represented each word, and then determinatives, denoting action, and homophones, denoting abstracts, were added to each principle sign. Hieroglyphs were written in continuous lines and were not divided by punctuation into words or sentences. Their essentially pictorial character made them very decorative, and often little details such as the feathers of a bird's wing, or the mottled skin of a snake are carved with great care on the stone. The magical nature of hieroglyphic writing was never entirely lost sight of, and sometimes a sign representing a dangerous creature such as a crocodile or snake would have been rendered harmless by severing the head or transfixing it with a knife or harpoon. Towards the end of the pharaonic period in the first millennium BC, the hieroglyphic system became more complicated and augmented by a number of new signs until in the Ptolemaic period, thousands of signs are found on the temple walls where the priestly scribes exercised their ingenuity in the invention of cryptographic writings that only they could read, thus nullifying the function for which written communication was invented. The last surviving hieroglyphic inscription is dated 395 AD, in the reign of the Roman emperor Theodosius.

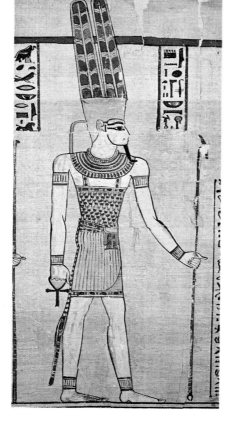

The Afterlife was of great importance to the ancient Egyptians and few people have devoted so much of their time and wealth to preparation for their death than they did. From the moment of his accession, a king started to plan and to build his tomb and the funerary temple attached to it, where his cult was to be perpetuated after his death. The wealth of officials and commoners, to a lesser degree, was also hoarded to provide suitable funerary equipment, the costly rite of mummification whereby the body was preserved, and the elaborate and costly funeral itself which might involve hundreds of participants, both priests and laymen. The afterlife was conceived of as continuation of life on earth and so the dead man would need, in his tomb, all those necessities and luxuries which made life on this earth pleasant. At the same time, the Egyptians were a realistic people and they had a very human fear of death; its inevitability was always before them.

How then did they reconcile the inevitable fact of death with the divinity of their king who, as a god, must be above death? The answer was to be found in the myth of the god Osiris who was believed once to have ruled Egypt as king. He was murdered by his brother Set, who seized the throne but was at last defeated by Osiris' son Horus; he avenged his father and became in turn king of Egypt. Osiris, the embodiment of vegetation which dies in winter and is resurrected in spring, lived on as lord of the Underworld and every king of Egypt therefore, after death, was thought to become Osiris and partake of his kingdom in the hereafter. The whole body of funerary beliefs were devised originally for the king's survival after death and he alone had expectation of eternal life in the company of the great gods. As time went on however, the nobles in his entourage, and then a large number of what might be called the middle class aspired to similar privileges in the hereafter; by the New Kingdom, 'the Osiris So-and-So' became the common designation for 'the late Mr So-and-So'. But Osiris was also the judge of the dead, and in the tombs of king and commoner alike, the deceased is shown in the presence of the divine Assessors before whom he had to account for his life on earth. The virtues which he claimed to possess and the sins which he repudiated, are those which the didactic literary texts copied by schoolboys also emphasize: patience and moderation, respect for age, generosity to the poor and oppressed, fair dealing and truthful speaking, are the virtues praised. In these teachings we glimpse a code of ethics not unlike those of the modern world.

The likeable character and gay temperament of the ancient Egyptians shines through their art and their literature, and is reflected in the bright colours of the ornaments they wore and the beauty of the objects of their daily use. Much in their religion may have been gloomy, even repellent, but an incurable optimism radiates even from the tombs and a sense of humour everywhere breaks through the solemnity. Above all, they held the firm belief that the sun shone on Egypt and the Nile flowed for the benefit of its people, and that the gods would care for them:

> *Hail to thee, Ra, Lord of Truth,*
> *whose sanctuary is hidden, lord of gods...*
> *who hears the prayer of him who is in captivity,*
> *who is kindly of heart when one calls upon him,*
> *who saves the weak from the strong, the meek from the*
>   *haughty,*
> *for love of whom the Nile comes*
> *Lord of Sweetness, great in love,*
> *at whose coming the people live.*

The modern science of Egyptology may be said to have begun with the Emperor Napoleon. With his expedition to Egypt in the early years of the nineteenth century came an army of French savants whose task was to record and to investigate the country's natural history and antiquities. The results of their researches were published in thirty six weighty volumes, and gave impetus to the exploration and study of Egypt's past. In the western Delta, at Rosetta, some soldiers discovered a very precious document: a decree, inscribed on a slab of black basalt, in Greek and also in two ancient Egyptian scripts, the hieroglyphic and the cursive demotic. This trilingual text provided scholars in several countries with their first clue to the decipherment of the Egyptian script and language. Among them were the Englishman, Thomas Young, and the Frenchman Jean-François Champollion whose knowledge of Coptic (the form of the ancient language still surviving in the liturgy of the Christian church in Egypt) helped him to elucidate several royal names mentioned in the decree and to deduce therefrom the principles on which the hieroglyphic system of writing was constructed. Champollion died in 1832 at the early age of 42, after only ten years of work on his great discovery, but others carried on his work and by the middle of the nineteenth century it was already possible to decipher and understand correctly many of the ancient texts and to compile grammars and vocabularies, and to write an outline history. Meanwhile antiquaries ransacked the ancient sites; much was discovered but in the absence of scientific methods of excavation much was lost, for the careless or ignorant investigator can destroy evidence in the course of his search.

In the year 1850 another young Frenchman, by the name of Auguste Mariette, was sent out to Egypt to buy Coptic manuscripts for the Louvre in Paris. Finding archaeology more to his taste than haggling for texts, he started to dig in the area of the great cemeteries at Saqqara, near the site of Memphis, once the capital of ancient Egypt. Traces of an avenue of sphinxes reminded him of a passage from the Greek writer Strabo 'There is also a Serapeum at Memphis in a place so sandy that the winds pile up the sands, beneath which we saw the sphinxes buried up to their heads.' Here then, argued Mariette, might be found the famous necropolis of the sacred Apis bulls, successive incarnations of a god whose popularity in Graeco-Roman times had brought pilgrims from far and near. Success rewarded his enthusiasm. He found the entrance, flanked with a semicircle of statues, and some months later penetrated into the vaults where the sacred bulls had been interred in huge granite sarcophagi.

The news of his discovery made newspaper headlines and he was permitted to continue his excavations. In 1858 he was given official status by the Khedive, as Conservator of Monuments, and his life was thenceforth dedicated to the excavation and preservation of the antiquities of Egypt. His successor, Gaston Maspero, carried on his work; to him was largely due the building of a Museum of Egyptian Antiquities worthy to house the huge number of works of art now enriching the national collections, and furnished with laboratories and workshops for their treatment and preservation. The science of Egyptology achieved popularity in Europe and America; learned societies were formed and expeditions sent out. Perhaps the most spectacular of all archaeological discoveries was that of the unplundered tomb of King Tutankhamun, found by Howard Carter after years of patient search. The importance of this find for the history of Egyptian art was immeasurable and its impact on the public was immediate; excitement grew as one treasure after another was brought to light. But it added little to the sum of knowledge of Egypt's history. The story had already been pieced together, bit by bit, through the painstaking work of philologists working on the texts and of archaeologists studying the material remains.

The soil of Egypt is not yet exhausted; it has more treasures to be unearthed. As recently as the years 1968-70 the late Professor W B Emery, excavating at Saqqara for the Egypt Exploration Society and the Egyptian Antiquities Service, discovered a labyrinth of galleries in one of which the sacred cows, the mothers of Mariette's Apis bulls, had been buried. The last chapter in the history of the civilization of Ancient Egypt has not yet been written.

Brief note: – Old Kingdom (2664-2155 BC) covered Dynasties III–VIII.
Middle Kingdom (2052-1786 BC) covered Dynasty XII.
New Kingdom (1554-1075 BC) covered Dynasties XVIII–XX.

Margaret Drower

I
CREATOR GODS, AND THE CENTRES OF RELIGIOUS THOUGHT

1

Plate 1

The two gods of the Nile shown here were really one god, Hapi, one of the few who was common to all Egypt and part of no theological system. He was invoked to ensure the annual flooding of the great river which made the fields fertile and fed the people. Hapi was represented with the body of a man, vigorous but fleshy, and with a woman's breasts, combining in one image both aspects of fertility.
The god on the left wears a crown of lotus plants; he represents the Nile in Upper Egypt. The one on the right, wearing a crown of papyrus, the Nile in Lower Egypt. The carving is a symbolic picture of the union of the two parts of Egypt – the two Hapis are binding the ties of lotus and papyrus. The carving comes from the pedestal beneath the huge statues of Rameses II in front of the great temple at Abu Simbel. Nineteenth Dynasty.

2

Plate 2

One of the most important documents to have
survived from the beginnings of Egyptian history
is the slate palette of King Narmer. The reverse,
shown here, depicts the king brandishing a mace
over a fallen captive – a victory motive that
occurs again and again in Egyptian art. Narmer was
a king of Upper Egypt who subdued Lower
Egypt and the Nile delta; the crown he wears
would later be combined with that of the defeated
people and produce the more familiar diadem which
the god Atum can be seen wearing in the next
picture. Particularly interesting here is the falcon
in the top right corner, leading a captive by the
nose and trampling on delta plants to signify
the subjugation of the region. The falcon is Horus,
and every succeeding pharaoh claimed to be his
earthly embodiment. The palette comes from
Hierakonpolis and is now in the Cairo Museum.
First Dynasty.

Plate 3

The three great pyramids seen through a dawn
haze. More than any other feature they epitomize
ancient Egypt in the minds of Europeans, and it was
probably no mere caprice on the part of the
pharaohs who built these tremendous tombs that
they should have taken their singular shape.
The religion of ancient Egypt was a synthesis,
developed over centuries, of the main elements of
total religions which arose in four different cities:
Heliopolis, Memphis, Hermopolis and Thebes.
A feature common to all of them was the belief
that life began on the primeval hill that rose out of
Nun – the primeval waters. The pyramids were
probably symbolic representations of the primeval
mound. The great pyramids are at Giza: the one
in the foreground is that of Mykerinus with, in
front, the small pyramids of three of his queens;
next is the pyramid of Khephren – which looks the
largest because it stands on higher ground than the
one behind it; the third is the greatest of all, that of
Kheops. The three pharaohs were of the Fourth
Dynasty.

3

4

Plate 4

Atum, the god of Heliopolis. His coming was interpreted in various ways: he formed himself out of his own will; he arose from the primeval waters; he came, and found nowhere to stand, so he created a hill (the primeval mound); he came out of the darkness, bringing light to the world. Since one of his names was Ra–Atum he was necessarily connected with the sun which was so important in the religion of ancient Egypt. He created more gods by mating with himself – the *Pyramid Texts* of the fifth century BC suggest that he was regarded as bisexual or, so to speak, both-sexual; the Egyptians saw the process of creation in sexual terms so the first god would logically be of both sexes. Atum here wears the *pschent* – the double crown of the pharaohs, and embraces the Twelfth Dynasty pharaoh Sesostris I. The Egyptian kings were fond of having themselves portrayed as the object of the gods' affections. Sesostris is on the left.

Plate 5

Shu, son of Atum and god of the air, who was born when his father spat him out. He can be seen in this portion of the papyrus of Pa-Shebut-n-Mut, who was a musician priestess of Amon-Ra in the Twenty-First Dynasty. The papyrus depicts the funeral rites of the priestess; the tiny figure on the extreme left is in fact a representation of her soul. Shu holds aloft the emblem of the sun-disk, and protects the soul on its voyage across the desert plateau, represented by the wavy lines of sand. On the right are the rudders of heaven and the eye of Ra. Atum also brought forth a daughter, Tefnut, sometimes described as a rain goddess but in the myths fulfilling the all-important place of a consort for Shu her brother. The papyrus is in the British Museum.

Plate 6

The rising sun supported by the air. At dawn the sun was likened to a scarab beetle rolling the sun before him just as a scarab beetle rolls a ball of dung. In this manifestation he was Khepri, seen here in the solar barque supported on the arms of Shu, while the sun itself is received by the sky-goddess Nut. The Egyptians believed that the ball pushed by the scarab beetle contained an egg, therefore the beetle was renewed of its own substance. So the scarab became identified with Atum the creator. The illustration is from a copy of the ancient Egyptian *Book of the Dead*, now in the British Museum.

5

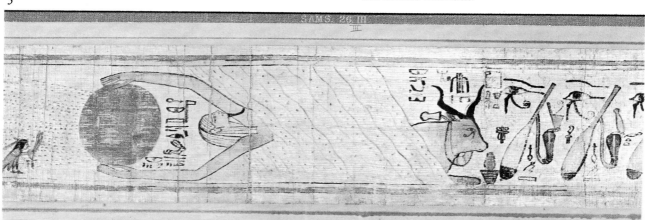

SAMS. 26 III

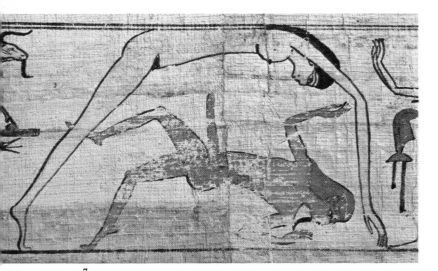

7

8

9

Plate 7

Shu and Tefnut became the parents of Geb, the earth, and his sister Nut, the sky. Another tradition has it that they were the children of Ra, the sun at full strength. Before the present world was made Geb and Nut were coupling and this for some reason aroused the wrath of Ra; he ordered Shu (as the god of air) to separate them, and with a great wind Shu complied. Nut was lifted off her recumbent lover and her body formed the arch of the sky. Geb, lying propped up on one elbow and with bent knee, formed the earth with its mountains and valleys. In this papyrus painting of the Twenty-first Dynasty he is seen to be green, the usual colour given to him as a vegetation god. The papyrus is in the British Museum.

Plate 8

As power shifted from city to city in the long course of Egyptian history the deities of the ascendant city assumed the leading place. Heliopolis was to give way to Memphis, and in time the centre of power was vested in Thebes, the city of the greatest pharaohs and the god Amon. Rameses II ruled from Thebes and he also built the great temples at Abu Simbel, where the tomb of his queen, Nefertari, was decorated with superb pictures of the gods. It can be seen that the older ones, like Atum, were never forgotten; the major figure here is Osiris since the painting is in a tomb – but the god on the right wearing the double crown is Atum. In his right hand he carries the *ankh*, the symbol of life. Nineteenth Dynasty.

Plate 9

The lion-headed Sekhmet receives offerings of lotus flowers from Imen-m-hebra and members of his family. This relief carving from a family tomb is now in the Cairo Museum and is notable for two reasons: it shows Sekhmet as the chosen deity of a family – not the role, the myths suggest, that she was most suitable for; and the offering of lotus flowers personifies her son Nefertum who completes the Memphis triad of gods (Ptah was his father). Sekhmet was the defender of the divine order, and she was sent forth as a lioness to chastise mankind on the occasion when they neglected to honour the gods. Unfortunately she set about the task with such relish that the supreme god had to intervene lest she destroy mankind completely.

10

Plate 10

A wall painting from the tomb of Sennofer
at Thebes. Sennofer was the keeper of the royal
gardens during the reign of Thuthmosis III, and
he is seen here with his sister, Merit, at his side.
He holds to his nostrils the lotus, the symbol of
rebirth and the personification of Nefertum whose
name means 'lotus'. Nefertum was a god of
Hermopolis, an ancient city to the south of Memphis
which gave many gods in their first form to
Egypt. He was adopted by the Memphis priests
to complete the triad and to stress his father
Ptah's role as the creator – it was apt that the
creator's son should symbolize rebirth. Eighteenth
Dynasty.

Plate 11

When King Narmer subdued Lower Egypt
he built a new capital for the united country.
The site he chose was at the apex of the Nile
Delta and the new city was called Memphis.
The high god of this region was Ptah, master
of destiny and creator of the world. The gods
of Heliopolis were, as far as the new city
was concerned, merely manifestations of him.
In this representation, a bronze statue now in the
British Museum, Ptah can be seen in his most
familiar form – that is with his legs and arms close
to his body. This is believed to be an indication of
his antiquity; his likeness was first fashioned before
men knew how to model arms and legs as
separate limbs. Memphis was a great trading centre
and the city's chief god, the patron of stonemasons,
metalworkers, boatbuilders, etc. was also the
Divine Artificer. Ptah was the rare example of an
Egyptian god who created by spiritual means
rather than physical; and while he never ceased to
command respect he was never a favourite with
ordinary people. He is seen carrying a composite
sceptre uniting the emblems of life, stability
and power.

25261

[25261]

11

12

Plate 12

The creation myths of Hermopolis, like those of Heliopolis and Memphis, speak of a primeval mound. At Hermopolis the main temple site stood near a sacred lake and in the lake was a small island – the primeval mound and a great place for pilgrimages. To this mound, in the time of chaos, came the celestial goose, the 'Great Cackler' who broke the silence of the universe. He laid an egg and from this was born Ra, sun god and creator of the world. (The shell from which he emerged was preserved at Hermopolis and shown to pilgrims). The Great Cackler was also the emblem of Geb, the Heliopolitan god of the earth, and can be seen in plate 7. The ancient traditions of Egypt were transferred happily from centre to centre; Amon of Thebes was also associated with the goose. The geese shown here are from a very ancient tomb at Maidum, and are now in the Cairo Museum. Third Dynasty, 2,600–2,500 BC.

13

Plate 13 and 14

Another bird which was said to have laid the cosmic egg was the ibis. This was a belief that held sway in Hermopolis and the god the ibis represented was Thoth. But a civilization which produced such a proliferation of beliefs inevitably produced a proliferation of traditions too – Thoth was also a god of Heliopolis; and another tradition, which said that Thoth was self-begotten and appeared at the beginning of time in a lotus flower, is attributed to the Hermopolitans. A god of wisdom, god of the moon, inventor of speech, patron god of scribes, the Divine Recorder – so many functions were attributed to him that it is evident that Thoth was a synthesization of a number of gods from various parts of Egypt who in their own region fulfilled these functions. One that is definitely identifiable is the ancient moon god Asten who was shown in the form of a baboon, a form in which Thoth was frequently depicted. His ibis form is shown in the bronze statue, his baboon form in a tomb painting from Tuna Gebel.

14

15

Plate 15

Lotus columns from the great temple at Thebes
(present–day Karnak). The great god of
Hermopolis was Ra, and the myth relates that a
lotus rose from the primeval waters. The lotus
flowered, and when its petals opened a child
was disclosed, borne on the calix, who was Ra.
Another version of his birth says that the flower
opened and revealed a scarab beetle, the symbol of
the sun. The beetle turned into a boy, who wept,
and his tears were mankind. The sun symbolism,
already noted in the story of Khepri, is explicit
here: the lotus is a flower which opens in the sun
and closes when the sun sets. Nineteenth Dynasty.

16

17

Plate 16 and 17

About 1,600 BC the centre of power in ancient Egypt shifted to Thebes, the site of which is now spread over the present-day Luxor and Karnak. Here also, as in the centres already described, there was a firm belief that everything began on the primeval mound: the city of Thebes stood on it, according to the priests. The ascendancy of Thebes occurred when recorded history in Egypt was already 2,000 years old and this enormous span of time had made it possible for the high gods of Heliopolis, Memphis and Hermopolis to be totally accepted by the people at large. The priests of the new capital, determined that its religious order should lead as effectively as the political, insisted that all other gods derived from the great god of Thebes, Amon, who until then had no more than local importance. Amon's first appearance in the world was in the head and skin of a ram – the creature which in that region had most importance as a symbol of fertility. The illustration shows the avenue of ram-headed sphinxes which led to the great temple of Amon at Thebes, and some of the tremendous columns of the hypostyle hall. These were twelve feet in diameter and nearly seventy feet in height; each one was elaborately carved. The hall was 330 feet long and 170 feet deep – but this enormous structure, an achievement to be compared with the building of the pyramids, is only one example of the grandeur of the Theban period. Each pharaoh, anxious for immortality, made a contribution of his own and sometimes enlarged and embellished the temples of his predecessors. Nineteenth Dynasty.

II
THE PRINCIPAL GODS

21

Plate 21

Ra, the sun god of Heliopolis, seen in an inlaid bronze aegis of the Ptolemaic period. Called the Father of the Gods, Ra once ruled on earth during a golden age when men and gods could live together happily. While he was in his full vigour the order of the universe seemed immutable but there came a time when even he, the supreme god, had to yield to another – the events recounted in the story of Horus and Set. Each morning Ra, as the sun, rose in the east and set off across the world, to sink below the horizon in the west. He was often shown as a disk, borne on a boat – the solar barque – but the most familiar representation was perhaps as a man with a falcon's head or as a falcon.

Plate 22

The adoration of Ra, from The *Book of the Dead* of Hunefer, now in the British Museum. The sun god appears over the eastern horizon and is received by seven figures of Thoth, in his form as a baboon. He carries on his head the solar disk with the uraeus symbol – the emblem of all the the pharaohs' power. In the lower half of the picture is the djed-column which represents Osiris; on the left is Isis and on the right is Nephthys. Early Nineteenth Dynasty.

Plate 23

A leaf from the papyrus of Ani, an Eighteenth Dynasty *Book of the Dead* in the British Museum. At the top of the leaf are two pictures of Ra proceeding on his journey. On the right the solar barque travels as the bright sun of day; the picture on the left shows the approach of night – the strength of the sun diminishes and the stars appear as the sky grows dark. Eventually the barque entered the realm of night and met the powers of darkness. The chief of these was the serpent Apep who tried to swallow the barque; a nightly struggle ensued, and when the sun reappeared on the eastern horizon the next day prayers of thankfulness were offered that Ra was triumphant and the sun would continue to shine. The sun god was often called Ra-Harakhte, or Horus of the Horizon: Horus was an early sun god always depicted as a falcon.

22
23

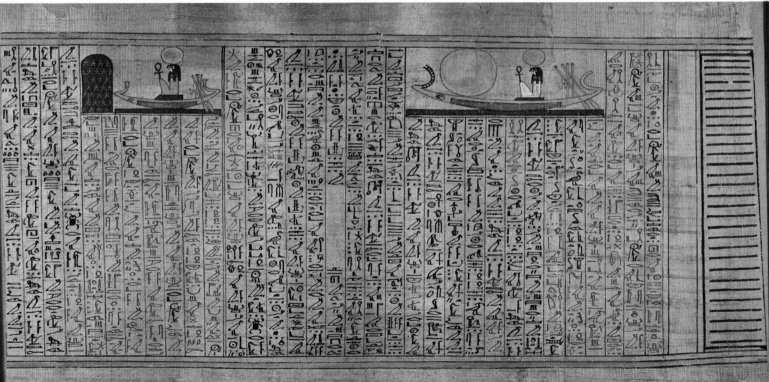

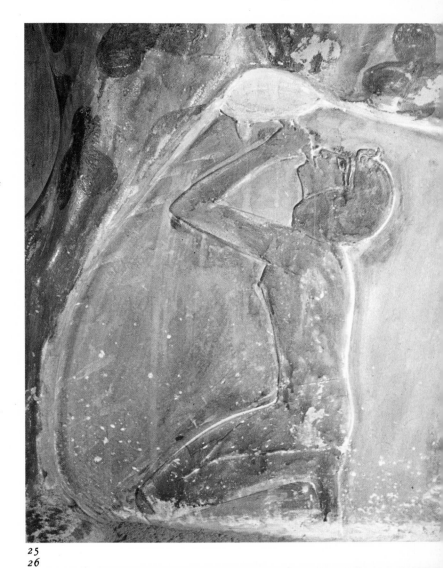

Plate 24

The sun god is frequently seen in copies of the *Book of the Dead* and in wall paintings from tombs and mortuary temples. This may seem odd since modern thinking does not normally connect a sun god with death. His presence in so many of them is explained by the tradition that Ra always sent his son Anubis to prepare the body of Osiris for burial, and by the fact that the sun sank over the western horizon at night – Ra-Harakhte showed the way to the world of the dead. This illustration is from the tomb of Nefertari, the queen of Rameses II, at Abu Simbel. On the left is the goddess Hathor, Ra's daughter, wearing on her head the sign of a falcon on a perch which meant the west where the dead were buried. On the right is Ra-Harakhte wearing the sun disk and uraeus, and holding the *ankh* in his right hand. Nineteenth Dynasty.

Plate 25 and 26

The goddess Hathor. An ancient sky goddess, she was first represented as a cow; later she was shown as a woman with a cow's head, and then simply as a goddess as in the preceding picture. In the myths she and Isis are often confused: Hathor in some traditions is the mother of Horus, though the stronger and more important myth of Isis and Osiris gives the mother's part to Isis. But confusion is further increased by the habit of some iconographers of portraying Isis with cow's horns. However the cow attribute is principally Hathor's and she was often described as the *nurse* of Horus, which led to the pictures of her as a cow suckling the pharaoh. The one thus engaged is Amenhotep II, in a wall painting from his tomb. Hathor was also believed to suckle the dead, to sustain them on their journey to the next world, a function depicted in the mural from the tomb of Rameses·VI in the Valley of the Kings. Hathor was the goddess of light-hearted pleasure and love, and of music and dancing.

25
26

27

Plate 27

Detail of a colossal statue of Rameses II at
Karnak, showing the pharaoh as the god Osiris.
(The pharaohs had no modesty whatever about
such matters, as the pictures in this book will
testify. In any case they believed themselves to be
the 'living' Horus; a great deal would follow
from that).

Osiris was an ancient fertility god with a
very widespread cult. The myths surrounding him
say that he was the son of Nut and Geb, and at his
birth the all-powerful Ra acknowledged him as his
heir. He brought civilization to Egypt and taught
the people how to cultivate the food plants. He was
married to Isis, his sister, and she ruled the
country with equal success whenever Osiris was
absent spreading his civilizing mission to other
peoples. The god Set was brother to Osiris;
Nephthys was his sister. Nineteenth Dynasty.

28

Plate 28

The goddess Isis holding a sistrum. This painted
relief is from a temple built at Abydos by the
pharaoh Seti I, the father of Rameses II. Isis was
most venerated as the wife of Osiris and the mother
of Horus but she had an equal reputation as the
Enchantress. Her magic was allied to the wisdom
of Thoth and given to mankind as a skill in healing;
she was also responsible, as the counterpart of
Osiris, for teaching the household arts to women.
She taught them weaving and spinning, and how
to grind the corn. Her strongest appeal was as the
sorrowing wife and devoted mother – every
woman could identify with her and she has been
seen by some commentators as the archetype of
a cult that continues in the Christian churches to
the present day.

Plate 29

A detail from a bronze statuette in the British Museum depicting Set, the brother of Osiris and the agent of his destruction. Set was one of the oldest gods of Egypt and, remarkably, retained his position as a deity while the myths credited him with every evil deed. He was jealous of the eminence of Osiris, and when the latter returned to to Egypt invited him to a banquet under the guise of friendship. Set imprisoned his brother in a chest lined with lead, and had the chest thrown into the Nile.

Plate 30

The chest was carried down to the sea and cast ashore on the coast of Byblos, where it lodged in the branches of a sapling. The sapling, growing into a tree, enfolded the chest, and eventually the tree was cut down and made into a beautiful column for the king's palace. Isis was able to divine where the chest was and she made her way to Byblos; she used her skills and her magic crafts to secure a place at court and was made nurse of the royal child. At night she became a swallow, flying round the beautiful column and mourning Osiris. (The picture is a detail from the painted coffin of Seni, *c* 2,000 BC, now in the British Museum). Isis also tried to give the royal child immortality by burning his mortal attributes; but the queen came upon her and screamed in terror which prevented the process from being completed. Isis revealed herself; she was given the chest from the column and allowed to go back to Egypt.

29

30

31

Plate 31

Isis hid the chest in the marshes of the Delta but
it was discoverd by Set when he was out hunting.
He smashed the chest and cut the body to pieces,
distributing them over a vast area; his hope was
that they could never be assembled and his revenge
would be complete. But Isis called on Set's wife,
the goddess Nephthys, to help her – Nephthys was
sister to both Isis and Osiris. The two roamed over
the land and painfully collected the pieces,
reassembling them to make the first mummy.

   This part of the Osiris myth became an
integral part of Egyptian burial rites, and can be
seen in this painting from the tomb of Sennutem,
a member of the royal household during the
Nineteenth Dynasty. Protecting the dead man are
those who mourned for Osiris – Isis and Nephthys,
in the form of kites.

32

Plate 32

Despite her great powers, Isis was unable to
bring Osiris back to life. Yet her gifts were
formidable enough to enable her to concieve a
child by him, and in due time Horus was born.
Set discovered this and soon Isis was aware that she
was watched constantly by her enemy, who
intended to kill the child when the opportunity
came. Isis, determined that her son should live to
take his father's place, invoked the protection of Ra,
who sent down Thoth from the solar barque.
The sun halted in the heavens and Isis was promised
that all would be well. Osiris remained a king – in
the other world, and all men in dying hoped
that they would aspire to his honoured company.
Osiris is seen here as the divine mummy, wearing
the *atef* crown. He carries the crook and flail,
symbols of royalty, and on either side are two
funeral sacrifices and two columns. The Eyes of Ra
look down on him and the lotus symbol of rebirth
stands before him. Painting from the tomb of
Sennutem. Nineteenth Dynasty.

33

Plate 33

Isis and Osiris. The divine couple portrayed on a
painted relief in the mortuary temple of the
pharaoh Seti I at Abydos. Osiris is seated and Isis
stands behind his chair. The pharaoh is behind
Isis, with his back to her, and overhead, in full
flight, is the vulture goddess Nekhebet. A protective
goddess of Upper Egypt, Nekhebet's function were
particularly associated with the monarchs; she can
be seen here holding the royal ring in her talons.
The relief is from the Horus shrine of the temple,
which is of the Nineteenth Dynasty.

Plate 34

Isis and Horus. Isis, wearing cow horns and the sun
disk, is suckling the infant Horus, who is oddly
represented as an adult pharaoh. Statues of Isis
were generally portraits of the reigning queen,
which is why the goddess is shown wearing the
uraeus. The infant Horus was sometimes portrayed
as a child wearing the pharaonic crown and with
a finger to his lips. This group is bronze, of the
Nineteenth Dynasty, and is now in the Abbey
Museum, New Barnet.

35

36

Plate 35

Isis, from the shrine of Tutankhamun. There was a tradition that she protected the dead Osiris with long feathery wings that, as the Great Enchantress, she was able to grow. Another says that it was with her wings that she attempted to transmit to him the breath of life. Inevitably, she was adopted as one of the protector goddesses in funeral rites and frequently depicted with her sister Nephthys, similarly winged, their plumaged arms entwined. Carved wood, overlaid with gold. Eighteenth Dynasty.

Plate 36

Like all the principal gods of Egypt – with the possible exception of Osiris – Horus had many forms. The god of ancient times seen on the palette of King Narmer brought the falcon's head, and the association with Ra the sun disk; but in addition to those forms there were local deities absorbed by him, and old gods who in some form represented the sun. One of these was Haroeris, or Horus the Elder, variously the son or husband of Hathor, and easily confused with the son of Isis and Osiris. Originally Haroeris was a god of light, whose eyes were the sun and moon. Sometimes there was no moon, of course, and Haroeris became the patron god of the blind. Bronze statuette of the Twenty-sixth Dynasty, now in the British Museum.

Plate 37

As Harmahkis, Horus personified the rising sun. The name means Horus on the Horizon. He is seen here in the most famous sculpture in the world, the great Sphinx at Giza which was carved out of the solid rock near the pyramid of Khephren. The height of the Sphinx is sixty-five feet, and is believed to be a portrait of Khephren himself. Harmakhis was believed to be not only the sun god rising but also the repository of great wisdom, and a symbol of resurrection. The pharaoh Tuthmosis IV, as a young prince, fell asleep in the shadow of the Sphinx, and dreamed that Harmakhis entreated him to clear away the sand that was building up and threatening to engulf him; the god would award him the throne of Egypt in return. A stele was later uncovered on the site which bore out the details of the story. Tuthmosis declared that he owed his throne to Harmakhis, and this was to have dramatic consequences for the succeeding pharaohs of the Eighteenth Dynasty. (see plate 64.) The Sphinx was carved during the Fourth Dynasty.

37

38

Plate 38

Horus as a falcon. The great sky god's statue stands in the court of his temple at Edfu in Upper Egypt. His close connection with the pharaohs is stressed by his headdress, the double crown of Egypt. As a child, Horus narrowly escaped being destroyed by Set, who had murdered his father Osiris. As a man, he claimed his father's rank and, further, the leadership of the gods when Ra (as Ra-Harakhte) grew old. Set contested this claim, and demanded that Horus should justify it in combat. Ra wanted Set, as the god with the most authority, to be his successor; but most of the gods favoured Horus. When some of them, with scant respect, pointed out to Ra that his shrines were empty he retired from the debate in a bad temper.

39

40

Plate 39

Nothing would induce Ra to rejoin the discussion
and the whole matter was halted. It was the
goddess Hathor who coaxed him out of his sulks;
she went to his arbour and performed a striptease.
This cheered him up and he returned to the meeting,
where he demanded that Set and Horus should
put their cases in an orderly way for due
consideration. The case for Set was strong, many
agreeing with him that the throne of Osiris was
too great a challenge for one as young as Horus.
The illustration is from the tomb of Rameses VI.
The goddess Hathor is seen holding the sun in one
hand and man in the other. Twentieth Dynasty.

Plate 40

Eventually the struggle was joined and Set, older
in cunning than Horus, came very close to being the
victor. But he lacked an ally to equal the one
Horus could call upon – the great Isis who was
determined that her son should inherit the throne
of Osiris. She guided him through every phase of
the struggle, and turned the tables on Set when,
under the pretence of peace-making, he attempted
to rape Horus, knowing that this would discredit
him in the eyes of the other gods. Isis knew that
Set had a great liking for lettuce, so she prepared
a dish of crisp green leaves. Set ate the dish with
pleasure – and conceived, to the great mirth of the
company when it became known. Isis had added
the seed of Horus to the lettuce leaves.
The great goddess is seen here in a painted relief
from the tomb of Amun-kher-khopsh, one of the
sons of Rameses III. She embraces Rameses, who
wears the blue *khepresh* or war helmet of the
pharaohs. Twentieth Dynasty.

41

Plate 41

In spite of his mother's help Horus never managed to defeat Set decisively, and in the end the gods decided to appeal to Osiris himself. Osiris rebuked the gods: he said that his son was the rightful heir, and that the very food eaten by man and gods depended on the good offices of Osiris. Ra scoffed at that, declaring that the food plants and food animals would have been on the earth if Osiris had never existed. Osiris returned that his authority could not be challenged; that everyone would eventually rest with Osiris when they passed to the West, the land of the dead where he was judge. This decided the issue and Horus thus inherited his father's place. He re-established the reign of Mayet – justice – which Osiris declared had been cast down. Set was given the charge of the wind and storms. Horus is seen with his father Osiris in this relief from a temple at Abydos of the Nineteenth Dynasty.

Plate 42

One of the gods who favoured the case of Horus was Anhur, a local deity from the country near Abydos who became associated with the Osiris cult. Variously the creative power of the sun and the warlike aspect of Ra, he was identified by the Greeks with Ares. Probably his right arm, upraised, originally carried a lance; some representations gave him a cord by which he led the sun. A popular god with ordinary people, Anhur was the 'Saviour' and the 'Good Warrior' who gave protection against enemies, both human and animal. As a war god, his cult became powerful in the New Empire (Eighteenth to Twenty-fourth Dynasties) and flourished for nearly sixteen centuries – right up to the end of the Ptolemaic period when Egypt came under the domination of Rome. Statuette of the Twenty-fifth Dynasty, now in the British Museum.

42

43

Plate 43

Thoth. The ibis-headed god seen in a painted relief from the temple of Amon at Karnak, pouring the water of life from a vase. In addition to his function as a moon god and the inventor of speech Thoth was credited with considerable magic powers, and these were called upon by Isis herself in the story of Horus and Set. He also invented writing, which gave him enormous power since all wisdom came to be placed in that which was written down, and the calendar – he was the divine regulative force. The divine scribe, he was present at all funeral rites, where his function was to record the deeds of the dead man before they were placed in the scales with the feather of truth. Thoth was identified with Hermes by the Greeks. Nineteenth Dynasty.

44

Plate 44

Anubis as a black jackal with a bushy tail; a striking representation from the tomb of Tutankhamun. It is carved from wood and varnished black, with gilded decorations and eyes of alabaster and obsidian. The origin of this god probably lay in the fact that jackals could always be heard howling in the desert to the west of the Nile at sunset. The west was where the sun sank each day, and where burials usually took place. The jackal was a despoiler, as well as being associated with death, so he was propitiated, and came to be regarded as the messenger from the other world. It wasn't long before he became a god and he was always associated with death; he supervized and performed the funeral rites of Osiris which fixed the form of such ceremonies in Egyptian religion. Eighteenth Dynasty.

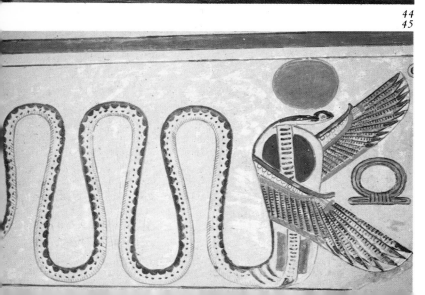

45

Plate 45

Buto, the cobra goddess. She is perhaps more familiarly depicted as the *uraeus* cobra worn in the pharaoh's crown, ready to deal death to his enemies. Her cult originated in the Delta and she was primarily a goddess of Lower Egypt just as the vulture goddess, Nekhebet, the other creature worn on the crown, was of Upper Egypt. Both goddesses were closely associated with the Nile. Buto was often to be seen on representations of Ra, and then she personified the sun's burning heat; she wears the sun disk in this painting from the tomb of the prince Amun-kher-khopsh in the Valley of the Kings. Twentieth Dynasty.

Plate 46

With their predilection for making gods of every animal they encountered the Egyptians naturally deified the crocodile, a creature familiar to people whose lives were spent by a great river and its Delta. The god was Sebek, a water god who was said to be the son of Neith. He became widely worshipped throughout Egypt after his rise to prominence in the Twelfth Dynasty (2,000 to 1,790 BC), when the pharaohs favoured the lakes and marshes of Lower Egypt. Another traditon that favoured him was that he was the form which Horus assumed when he searched for pieces of his father Osiris' body in the waters of the Nile. As a state god in the Twelfth Dynasty he became identified with the sun, and when Ra was identified with Amon after the rise of Thebes representations of Sebek began to appear with him wearing Amon's insignia – the ram's horns and the plumed headdress. Bronze of the Twenty-second Dynasty, now in the British Museum.

46

Plate 47

The ram was, according to the evidence of archaeology, one of the sacred beasts of the prehistoric people of the upper Nile. The creature occurs frequently in the iconography of Egypt but only Amon's representative bears a ram's form we can all recognize – an indication of his late ascendancy. Amon himself was said to have remained hidden until the times were ready for him; that is until the princes of Thebes, where he was a local deity, were ready to assume the hegemony of Egypt and make their city the capital. Their god became the great god Amon and soon all powers were ascribed to him; those of Ptah, of Ra, and of course of the erstwhile creator gods. Eighteenth Dynasty.

47

48

Plate 48

The goddess Mut. She was a local deity of the Thebes region, like Amon, and was the divine mother. Originally a vulture goddess, she was inevitably confused with Nehkebet; when she began to be portrayed as a woman the vulture was placed in her crown. She was a convenient goddess for the Thebans to have around – it was a simple matter to make her the consort of Amon. Their marriage was celebrated annually and on those occasions Amon made oracular pronouncements through his priests. The Greeks identified Mut with Hera. Nineteenth Dynasty sculpture, now in the Cairo Museum.

49

50

Plate 49

Mut can also be seen in this papyrus painting, partially obscured, standing behind Khons. The moon god of Thebes, he was the third member of that city's triad of gods; his mother was Mut and his father Amon. Here he wears the double-plumed crown of Amon. The myths surrounding him say that he was actually the afterbirth of Amon; the all-powerful sun being Amon, everything that pertained to him must have been divine, so the afterbirth became the moon. But two traditions are obviously in conflict here, since he was generally accepted as Amon's son. With Thebes in the ascendant, Khons assimilated the functions of Thoth – as the divine regulator – and of Shu – as god of the heavens and the atmosphere.

Plate 50

Amon giving his protection to the queen-pharaoh Hatshepsut. By the time of the Eighteenth Dynasty Amon was supreme; but, as we shall see, it was during the Eighteenth Dynasty that he was nearly overthrown. However, he survived the religious revolution and became even more powerful in the Nineteenth and the greatest pharaoh of that dynasty, Rameses II, acknowledged his might unequivocally. Amon was the god of victory, king of the gods, Lord of the Thrones of the World – all his titles were a recognition of Egypt's greatness during the Eighteenth Dynasty; stretching from the Euphrates to the Sudan, it was the greatest power of the ancient world. Nevertheless, in spite of all the power and grandeur associated with his name, Amon was a popular god with the people, who saw him as the protector of the poor and the weak.

Plate 51

Bast, the cat goddess, was a very ancient deity; she has been identified in the antiquities of the Second Dynasty – that means that she was worshipped as long ago as 3,200 BC. Her cult was in the Delta, at the city of Bubastis, and the pharaohs of the Twenty-second Dynasty, deciding to rule from there, made her a state deity. Bubastis was enriched and a new temple to Bast was built at Thebes. Her origins may have lain in the fact that the people of the Delta – a region frequented by snakes of many kinds – welcomed the wild cat, a killer of snakes, into their homes. The cat took readily to domestication. One myth says that Bast accompanied the solar barque through the regions of night, and nightly gave battle to the serpent Apep, the enemy of Ra. There was a cemetery of mummified cats at Bubastis which was noted by Herodotus in the second book of his *Histories*. Bronze of the Twenty-second Dynasty.

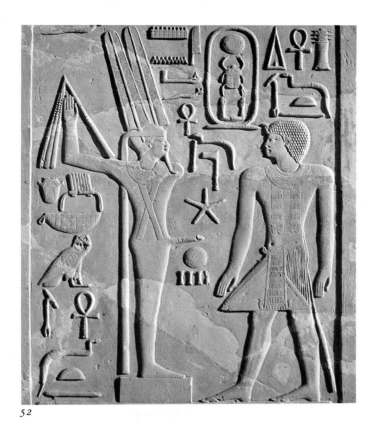

52

Plate 52

A Twelfth Dynasty relief carving from Thebes showing Sesostris I and the god Min. A god of fertility, Min was particularly the bestower of sexual powers in men, and at Abu Simbel a number of murals feature him being offered lettuce by the pharaoh; lettuce was believed to be an aphrodisiac in ancient Egypt and it was fed regularly to the white bulls (the sacred animals of Min) during the harvest celebrations. Min was the bringer of rain, and the generative force in nature – particularly he was associated with the growth and ripening of grain. At Thebes he was often shown wearing the crown of Amon and carrying a flail in one hand.

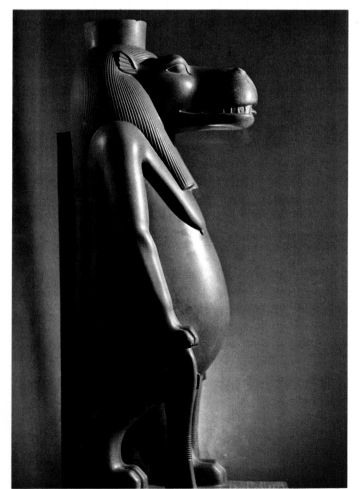

Plate 53

Taueret was a mother goddess of prehistoric times, and in spite of her grotesque association with the hippopotamus she was always revered as the protective deity of expectant mothers and of women in childbirth. Through later myths she acquired connections with the daily reappearance of Ra in the solar barque but her real strength lay in her role as a domestic goddess. Amulets of Tauret were placed in tombs to invoke her protection when the deceased was reborn in the kingdom of the dead.
Her connection with Ra was also one of rebirth – the sun reborn every day on the eastern horizon.
Here she is seen with the *sa*, the symbol of protection, in her right hand. Twenty-sixth Dynasty statuette from Thebes, now in the Cairo Museum.

Plate 54

Bes, the dwarf god who brought happiness to the home. He first appeared in Egypt in the Twelfth Dynasty (2,000 - 1,790 BC), and is believed to have originated in the Sudan; he is sometimes shown wearing a lion or leopard skin. The protector of the family, he was a friend to all women; he presided over their toilet, marriage, and at childbirth was on hand to drive away evil spirits. He was a merry god who danced and made music and in imitation of this his festivals were always gay occasions. He was most frequently depicted on head-boards of beds – particularly of marriage beds – and he is seen here as the terminal of an elaborately carved staff of the Twenty-first Dynasty.

54

Plate 55

Selket was originally one of the protective goddesses of the four sources of the Nile. These arose from the nether regions, and eventually Selket became one of the guardian goddesses at burials; she is seen here at one of the most famous in the world, that of the young pharaoh Tutankhamun. Her place was at the south-east side. Selket has been traced to prehistoric times and she was a goddess of fertility as well as a guardian and probably her association with the scorpion dates from then. Like the jackal, the scorpion was feared, so it was propitiated; from there to being made a deity was a short step for the Egyptians. The statue is carved from wood, and gilded. Eighteenth Dynasty.

55

Plate 56

Mayet, the goddess who personified justice and truth, who stood between illusion and reality, good and evil. When she was not honoured chaos came again.

Mayet was probably an abstraction, rather like Themis in Greek religion, but once she was named she was inevitably personified and the Egyptians regarded her as the daughter of Ra. She emerged with him from the primeval waters and replaced chaos; she was the light that Ra brought to the world. The pharaohs claimed to rule by Mayet and the ordinary people had a strong awareness of her; she was perhaps more important to them, who were ruled, than to those who ruled. Both pharaoh and commoner alike, however, knew that they would have to account to her when they died, and that their hearts would be balanced against her. (See plate 88.) Only if the scales were even would they be allowed into the presence of Osiris. The goddess is, always recognized by her ostrich plume – sometimes only the plume is present in the scales in the Hall of Judgment. Mayet is also to be seen in the barque of the sun, accompanying her father Ra. Painted relief from the tomb of Seti I, Nineteenth Dynasty.

56

III
THE LORDS OF THE TWO LANDS

57

Plate 57

The rulers of Egypt, while they represented themselves as gods on earth, never attained the status in myth of their counterparts in Greece. Their lives and deeds are well documented and this, paradoxically, kept them 'earthbound' in a way that never happened to the Greeks. The pharaohs could insist on their divine particulars but, in the end, it could be seen that this was merely what they said of themselves. Nevertheless they are a part of Egypt's mythology, since one cannot encounter the gods without also meeting the all-powerful rulers who glorified them. At Saqqara, near the step pyramid of the pharaoh Dhoser, we see a frieze of cobra heads. There is a tradition that during the conflict between Horus and Set the latter succeeded in tearing out Horus' eyes; the *uraeus* symbol replaced them and became thereafter the symbol of royal power. Third Dynasty.

58

Plate 58

Khephren, the pharaoh who built the second pyramid, and then ordered the Sphinx to be carved from the rest of the rock. This statue, one of twenty-three which were found in the hall of the Temple of Khephren, has a lonely majesty that strongly suggests the god-king. The god Horus, as a falcon, can be seen perched behind him, transmitting his strength to his representative on earth. The statue is of green diorite. Fourth Dynasty.

59

60

Plate 59

Sesostris I is received into the embrace of the god Ptah (see the picture in plate 4, where Sesostris is embraced by the god Atum). Ptah is the figure on the left. Sesostris I favoured Heliopolis and built a great temple there but his family came from the region of Thebes and he did not neglect to honour that city. This relief came from there, part of a temple he built when he honoured the main gods of Egypt and was received into their shrines as their son. It was in his reign that a hitherto obscure god of the Theban region, Amon, began to come to the fore. The temple built by Sesostris was demolished to make way for the great temple of Amon and the relief, nearly nine feet high, became part of a heap of rubble. It is now in the Cairo Museum. Twelfth Dynasty.

Plate 60

The Valley of the Kings on the west bank of the Nile at Thebes. The pharaohs of the Eighteenth, Nineteenth and Twentieth Dynasties had their tombs there, cut out of the rock in a defile in the mountains. Some of the burial chambers were over 600 feet deep in the rock, and contained many halls and chambers; but in spite of the most elaborate complications for sealing the tombs – and curses to any who disturbed them – not a single royal burial place was ever found to be completely intact. Even the celebrated tomb of Tutankhamun, with its fabulous treasures, showed signs of having been disturbed, and it should be remembered that Tutankhamun was far from being a monarch of any significance. What the tombs of Tuthmosis III, Amenophis III, or Rameses II would have contained can only be guessed at. They were successfully plundered, with scores of others, through the centuries.

61

Plate 61

The mortuary temple of Hatshepsut, the first woman to succeed completely in reigning over Egypt as a sovereign in her own right.
A matriarchal system of inheritance persisted in Egypt from the earliest times, and the throne could be gained by marriage to a royal heiress. Hatshepsut was the daughter of Tuthmosis I, and while she acknowledged that her brother – and husband – had a right to the throne and saw him reign as Tuthmosis II, she believed her own claim to follow him to be stronger than that of her half-brother who eventually reigned as Tuthmosis III. She had no compunction about declaring herself the daughter of the god Amon, and his priests must have agreed – the people did not question their pronouncements. This female pharaoh had elaborate reliefs carved in the temple, picturing in detail her direct descent from the god. Her successor took care to have the reliefs and their accompanying inscriptions chiselled out.

Plate 62

Tuthmosis as pharaoh, the third of his name.
The god who was invoked by Hatshepsut to help her gain the throne was, apparently, a fickle one. It was with the help of the priesthood of Amon that Tuthmosis III deposed his half-sister. Though she was an able ruler, she earned her half-brother's undying hatred in her scorn of him. The daughter of the first Tuthmosis, the sister and wife of the second, she had reason to be proud; her half-brother was merely the child of one of her brother – husband's 'other' wives. But the despised prince turned the tables on her with an oracle from the priests of Amon, which proclaimed his right to the throne. He went on to greatness – Egypt under Tuthmosis III reached its greatest extent and colossal wealth flowed in from the conquered countries.

62

63

Plate 63

Toward the end of his reign Tuthmosis III tired of the authority of Amon; that is, he tired of the priests of Amon, and began to look to another god to balance their power. To this end he planned a temple in Thebes to the east of the Temple of Amon, a temple to the rising sun. It was to contain a single obelisk, a great needle of stone inscribed to Ra-Harakhte, the Horus of the Horizon. This revolutionary step – in the city of Amon – was carefully ignored by his successor; Tuthmosis died before the temple was completed and the obelisk lay disregarded by the sacred lake of Thebes. The new pharaoh, Amenophis II, is seen here in a painting from his tomb in the Valley of the Kings. He faces Osiris, who offers him the breath of life in the *ankh* symbol.

Plate 64

At Medinet Habu, near Thebes, there can be seen the two colossal seated statues of Amenophis III. These are all that remain of the pharaoh's mortuary temple and their size – they are over sixty feet high – give some idea of what the temple could have been like in extent. The statues were carved from quartzite brought 400 miles from a quarry near Heliopolis. The reign of Amenophis III was one of splendour – Egypt was enjoying her supreme place in the ancient world; but the seed sown by Tuthmosis III had taken root and the old order was already being eroded. Despite the adherence of Amenophis II to the old ways his successor, Tuthmosis IV, had disturbed things further (see Plate 37). Harmakhis and Ra-Harakhte were aspects of the sun, and Amenophis III was sympathetic to the new beliefs. The ram-headed god was being ousted from his supreme place.

64

Plate 65

The revolution came with the next pharaoh, Amenophis IV. When he ascended the throne the great Eighteenth Dynasty was at its peak; when he died it was not only virtually over but sunk very low indeed. Amenophis IV pushed the idea of the sun as the supreme god farther than his predeccessors ever dreamed; the sun at its zenith, the bestower of all things was to be the *only* god. The pharaoh would naturally be his only representative – through the one god he would be immortal. The new god was *Aten* (disk), and Amenophis changed his name to Akhenaten. The statue shown here is in the Cairo Museum and represents a departure in the portrayal of the pharaohs. Ahkenaten refused to have his portraits idealized, and he was a sickly and far from comely man. Nevertheless he was shown in the Osiris position in this statue, with his arms crossed over his chest and carrying the crook and flail. It dates from the beginning of his reign, and originally stood in the temple to Ra-Harakhte which was begun by Tuthmosis III.

65

66

Plate 66

Akhenaten built a new city for his god lower down the Nile and called it Akhetaten. The site is close to the modern Tell el Amarna. The cult of the *aten* lasted about as long as the reign of the pharaoh who promoted it, about seventeen years. A wiser ruler might have been able to maintain his power while carrying out his religious reforms but history shows that Egypt suffered acutely in prestige during his reign. Akhenaten declared that he ruled by Mayet (the goddess personifying truth and justice) but his adherence to his personal ideals did not prevent the eroding of Egypt's frontiers or the growing unrest in Thebes, where the cult of Amon was actively persecuted. In any case, monotheism was an alien concept to the Egyptians, as we have seen. This stele from the Cairo Museum shows Akhenaten and his queen presenting offerings to Aten, who bestows the breath of life. The small figure behind the queen is one of the royal princesses, Meritaten.

67

68

Plate 67

Akhenaten's queen was Nefertiti, and her portrait busts show that she was a woman of remarkable beauty. The available evidence suggests that she was not an Egyptian – a striking departure for the Egyptian royal house which, to keep the line pure and to follow the example of Isis and Osiris, usually married the princes and princesses to each other. But her origins cannot be ascertained and some authorities maintain that her beauty represents to the full the ideal seen in so many of the Tombs of the Eighteenth Dynasty. Her ultimate fate is wrapped in mystery – she disappears from the visual records at some time in the last three years of the reign. This unfinished bust, itself a thing of beauty, comes from Tell el Amarna and is now in the Cairo Museum.

Plate 68

The death of Akhenaten was also the death of Aten as a god of any consequence. Amon resumed his supremacy in Thebes and order was restored to Egypt. Tutankhaten was given a more suitable name, and history knows him as Tutankhamun. A boy of nine, he was carefully prepared for his coronation by the priests of Amon and the officers of state, and of the gods he acknowledged as being present when he received the crown it was Amon who placed his hand on the king's neck – or so the ritual declared. The illustration shows the front panel of a painted chest from the tomb of Tutankhamun and commemorates a war against Syria during his reign.

Plate 69

Tutankhamun died when he was eighteen or twenty – the records are not clear – and was fated to become the most famous pharaoh in history. His life was unremarkable and his death was probably expected; neither of his predecessors was exactly robust and Tutankhamun's physical condition would have been known to his advisors. Tutankhamun is seen here in one of his funerary masks, a priceless object of beaten gold decorated with faience. He wears the *nemset* headdress and on his brow the protective goddesses Nekhebet of Upper Egypt and Buto of Lower Egypt. The treasures of his tomb, discovered in 1922, were what made the boy pharaoh famous; he himself could have been described, until then, as the most obscure of all the monarchs of Egypt.

70

Plate 70

The goddess Isis watches eternally. Her place was at the north-west, and three more of these exquisite gilded images were found in Tutankhamun's tomb. Selket, the scorpion goddess, had her place at the south-east, Nephthys at the south-west, and Neith at the north-east.

71
72

Plate 71

After Tutankhamun the Eighteenth Dynasty was virtually over, he was in fact the last of the legitimate line. The great god of Thebes, however, seemed eternal; Amon was as strong as he had ever been. Two pharaohs followed Tutankhamun in the Eighteenth Dynasty; Ay, who had been the vizier of Amenophis III, and Horemheb, a resolute soldier who gave Egypt a period of internal stability and peace. When he died one of his generals, Rameses, stepped into the vacant place and the Nineteenth Dynasty began. In this period Egypt recovered some of her former glory, particularly under Seti I. His successor was Rameses II, who left a display of stupendous glory that concealed for a time the fact that Egypt was truly in decline. The illustration shows a cartouche from the temple of Amon at Karnak, bearing the name, in heiroglyphics, of Rameses II.

Plate 72 and 73

Rameses II was the most vigorous builder of all the pharaohs and much of his construction was to his own glorification. The colossal seated statue is at Luxor; he wears the double crown of Egypt and the *uraeus* of the cobra goddess Buto. The four seated statues are all of the pharaoh, the facade of the famous rock temples at Abu Simbel before they were moved to save them from the rising waters of the Nile. The size of the statues is almost as stupendous as the pharaoh's conceit – the small figure in the upper centre is a mere god, Ra Harakhte, the guardian of the temple. Each one of the statues is sixty-five feet high.

74
75

Plate 74

A detail from Abu Simbel, showing the statue of the pharaoh which stands on the right of the entrance. The small figure which stands no higher than Rameses' knee is his wife Nefertari – who was also his daughter. On the side of the statue are carved the gods of the Nile.

Plate 75

The interior of the temple at Abu Simbel is adorned with coloured reliefs which show Rameses II in the company of the gods and goddesses. Here he is with Mut, the goddess who was the consort of Amon and who, with Khons, formed the Theban triad. It is interesting to note that the deities were always shown as resembling the pharaoh and as something like the same age. Rameses II is a young man here; no doubt the image of himself he wished to perpetuate. The gods who embrace the boy pharaoh Tutankhamun in the statues and reliefs which survive from his reign are clearly seen to be adolescent.

Plate 76

Nefertari had a tomb of her own – a beautiful one near present-day Luxor. The illustration shows the entrance to the sarcophagus chamber, into which a guide proceeds with his lantern. Mayet, the goddess of truth and justice, spreads her protective wings across the lintel, and the names and titles of the queen are depicted on the sides of the doors: Great Royal Wife, Mistress of the Two Lands, Nefertari.

76

Plate 77

A portrait of Nefertari, from her tomb. The The smaller temple at Abu Simbel is also hers, and dedicated to the goddess Hathor. The name Nefertari meant Beautiful Friend (or Companion) and the evidence suggests that she kept a permanent place in her husband's affections though she was his daughter and had been married to him before he attained the throne. Her mummy was not in the tomb when it was discovered and has never been traced. It is not known when she died.

Plate 78

Even when the pharaohs were no longer Egyptian they built fine temples to the country's gods. These would be dedicated to the deity in favour – the one the pharaoh believed had shown him especial grace. The Ptolemies, a dynasty of pure Greeks who ruled Egypt for nearly 300 years after the death of Alexander the Great, built two of particular interest, both of them to honour aspects of Horus. One was at Edfu on the Upper Nile, the other was even farther south, at Kom Ombo, and the ruins can be seen here, glowing in the setting sun. It was a twin sanctuary, to Horus the Elder (Haroeris) and the crocodile god Sebek.

77
78

IV
THE AFTERLIFE

79

Plate 79

A detail from the *Book of the Dead* of Ani, a scribe of the Eighteenth Dynasty.
With his wife Tutu he is shown making offerings to Osiris; the table is heaped
with fruit, bread and vegetables. Tutu carries a sistrum in one hand and wears on
her head a lotus flower, the symbol of rebirth.
The officers of the pharaoh's household were probably the only class in Egypt
who could afford elaborate tombs and many of them, especially those of the
Eighteenth Dynasty, proved to be enormously rewarding to the scholars. Ani was
probably one of the scribes of Amenophis III. The papyrus of his *Book of the Dead*
is now in the British Museum.

Plate 80

Osiris in the Hall of Judgment. As the supreme judge of the dead he is often shown as a mummy, either seated or standing. The Egyptians were primarily an agricultural people and like all such associated death and fertility – one was a beginning which arose out of its necessary end, the end in turn carried the seeds of another beginning. The origins of Osiris as a fertility god are remembered in the habit of portraying him with a green face. He carries the crook and flail, the twin symbols of royalty of Upper and Lower Egypt, and wears the *atef* crown. Most of our evidence for the funerary rites comes from the elaborate tombs of the powerful; nevertheless Osiris was a god for all, even the humblest, since he represented hope of another and perhaps better life after this one. Wall-painting from the tomb of Nefertari. Nineteenth Dynasty.

80

Plate 81

Seker, the god pictured as a sparrow-hawk, was originally a god of the dead in the religious system of the Old Kingdom with its capital at Memphis. He became identified with the Osiris cult when it spread throughout Egypt and later with Osiris himself. His original function was as the guardian of the entrance to the next world; he later became the guardian of the tomb. This representation comes from Kom Ombo during the Ptolemaic period, where he guards the sarcophagus itself.

81

Plate 82

As noted in other illustrations, burials took place in the west where the sun set, and this often meant a journey across the Nile. A funeral barque is depicted in this painting from the tomb of the pharaoh Seti I at Abydos. The dead man is shown as a mummy, and accompanying him is the serpent goddess Mertseger. She was known as the Mistress of the West and her name meant 'Beloved of him who makes the silence'; that is, Osiris. A desert goddess, she gave protection against the serpents of that region and was, particularly, the deity of the Theban necropolis. Nineteenth Dynasty.

82

83

Plate 83

The *ka* of the dead Ani. This was the transcendent part of a human being which, when he died, arose from him and travelled to the West. There the *ka* would be received by the goddess Hathor who provided refreshment, and by its heavenly self. The tomb was called the house of the *ka* and there it returned to dwell. The family of the deceased was very careful to provide nourishment for the *ka*; notwithstanding its possession of a heavenly self it was also a part of man and could perish if it lacked subsistence. In this leaf from the papyrus of Ani the *ka* is seen, left, rising from the body of the dead man and, right, at its station in the tomb.

84
85

Plate 84

Osiris, in the judgment hall, was attended by Isis and Nephthys and the four sons of Horus who were seated in front of his throne. Horus had numerous wives in his various aspects but these were usually believed to be his children by Isis, his mother – the Egyptians would have seen nothing wrong in that. They were appointed by their father as the guardians of the four cardinal points, and during the period when the viscera of the dead were removed during mummification they were also guardians of the jars which contained them. The human-headed Imset guarded the south and the jar containing the liver; the ape-headed Hapy guarded the north and the jar containing the lungs; falcon-headed Qebehsenuf guarded the west and the jar containing the intestines, and jackal-headed Duamutef the east and the jar containing the stomach. From the tomb of Nefertari, Nineteenth Dynasty.

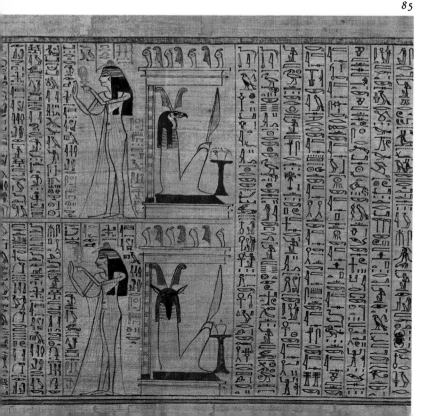

Plate 85

Anhai was a priestess and musician of Amon at Thebes toward the end of the Twentieth Dynasty. Her *Book of the Dead* is a beautiful and explicit document which charts the progress of the deceased Anhai to the hoped-for rebirth in the kingdom of Osiris. She would have been furnished with her *Book of the Dad* when placed in her coffin; it contained the ritual prayers that would carry her safely across the dreaded Nowhere between the living and the dead and see that she arrived safely in the Hall of Judgment. Then she would be conducted into the presence of Osiris by Anubis or Horus – Horus in this case.

Plate 86

When the funeral procession arrived at the tomb the ceremony of 'The Opening of the Mouth' was performed. This was a ritual remembrance of the visit of Horus to his father Osiris when he was able to take him the news that his murder had been avenged; that Set had been defeated and the son had attained his rightful place. In a much older tradition it had been Set who had given the gods their power to command – he had 'opened their mouths'. Horus could now perform the service for his father, which consisted of touching his lips with a ceremonial adze. Thus was the resurrection of the soul of Osiris achieved. The ceremony was performed in funerals to ensure that the way was open for the rebirth of the soul of the deceased. From the papyrus of Hunefer, Nineteenth Dynasty.

87

Plate 87

In the presence of Osiris the deceased would make a declaration of purity, that he or she was never guilty of evil, and that by addressing each of the gods boldly by name could prove that they were without sin. The proceedings were recorded by the Divine Scribe, the ibis-headed god of wisdom Thoth. The illustration is from the rock temple at Abu Simbel, and the pharaoh Rameses II is shown between Ra-Harakhte, whom he is presumably addressing, and Thoth.

Plate 88

The protestations of the deceased were the first part of the judgment but not the part that really mattered. The first part was almost a ritual incantation, a process of declaring something firmly in the hope of making it so in fact. But the truth would have to be satisfied in the end, and here Anhai is conducted to the final test. In the Hall of Judgment was a balance, and a tall staff surmounted by the symbol of Thoth as a baboon. Ibis-headed Thoth stood ready to record the outcome, and Horus led the deceased to the last trial. The balance was kept by jackal-headed Anubis, the conductor of souls, and waiting by him stood the monster Ammut, part lion and part crocodile, the Devourer. Anubis the heart of the deceased on one side of the balance, and the figure of Mayet on the other. The heart was believed to be the seat of intelligence and if innocent of evil it would balance with truth.

88

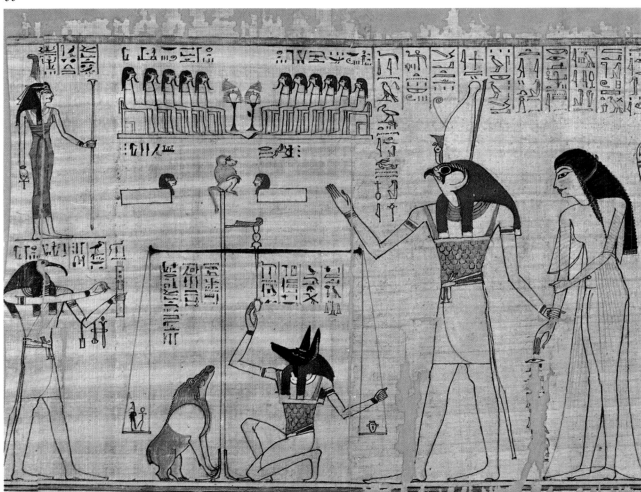

Plate 89

The verdict was recorded by Thoth, who wrote
the result on his tablets. If the heart and truth did
not balance each other the grim monster Ammut
was ready to devour the heart; that is, the
deceased. If the heart was innocent of evil the
goddess Mayet, seen here as a small figure in green,
garlanded the deceased with the feathers of truth and
they were then conducted to the throne of Osiris.
Anhai is shown as having passed the crucial test,
and this was not necessarily a presumption on her
part. Rather it was a hope expressed.

Plate 90

The life in the next world that every Egyptian
hoped for. On the right is Osiris, seated, and
before him a ritual sacrifice. Isis and Nephthys
stand behind his throne. Anhai, pure of heart, would
have been offered refreshment at the request of
Horus and granted the gift of living forever.
Osiris would allow her to depart and mingle freely
with the gods and the rest of those who enjoyed
his kingdom, and assign to her a place of her own.
In the centre is Anhai, about to begin her next life;
she is garlanded with vine leaves. In her new world
she will cherish the place assigned to her and in the
centre parts of the left picture she can be seen there,
enjoying what looks like pastoral bliss.

89

90

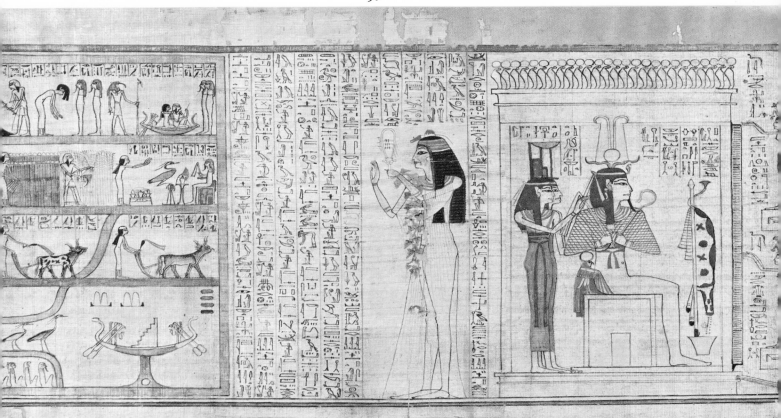

V
SACRED ANIMALS IN EGYPT

91

Plate 91

Ancient Egypt was a country which stretched from the mildly tropic shore
of the southern Mediterranean to the roasting heat of the Tropic of Cancer.
The great river flowed from beyond the mountains in the south and spread into a
many-channelled Delta in the north; on either side of it lay harsh and
inhospitable deserts. The range of animal life known to the ancient Egyptians
must have been great, and it must be borne in mind that civilization there can
be traced far back beyond 5,000 years. Man has always looked to the creatures
around him to express or personify a particular belief, and in predynastic times
in Egypt the gods would very likely have been tribal fetishes which took the
form of animals. Many of these made the transition into the form of a god, and
this humorous wall painting from the tomb of the pharaoh Seti I shows us a few
of them. Nineteenth Dynasty.

Plate 92

A detail from the painted coffin of Denytenamun, who was a priest of Amon in Thebes in the Twenty-first Dynasty. The bull wearing the *atef* crown is Apis; he was known as the life of Ptah, the creator god of Memphis. Ptah was, in some traditions, incarnate in a black bull brought to life by a moonbeam and this bull was given divine honours for a period of twenty-five years. Then it was slain – lest it show the debility of old age and bring weakness to the land – and embalmed, and buried with elaborate rites. At the moment of death the new Apis was born: he was looked for throughout the land, and always found, identified by the markings the priests knew.

Plate 93

Excavations proceeding at Saqqara, where every year new discoveries are made; the site, near that of Memphis, seems inexaustible. It was here, as long ago as 1851, that the Serapeum – the necropolis of the Apis bulls – was discovered, containing sixty-four mummified bulls. Apis was a fertility god and his name was a version of Hapi, the god of the Nile. As a fertility god he was bound to be associated with Osiris sooner or later, and this led to the name Serapis (Osiris–Apis). The association was further stressed by the continued renewal of Apis from death to life. The living bull was installed in a courtyard of the temple of Ptah at Memphis; the dead bull was mourned for sixty days before being embalmed and buried in the Serapeum in a huge sarcophagus.
The Serapeum was built in the Eighteenth Dynasty, and from that time the lives of the bulls were carefully recorded. The centre of the Apis cult was moved to Alexandria during the time of the Ptolemies.

92

93

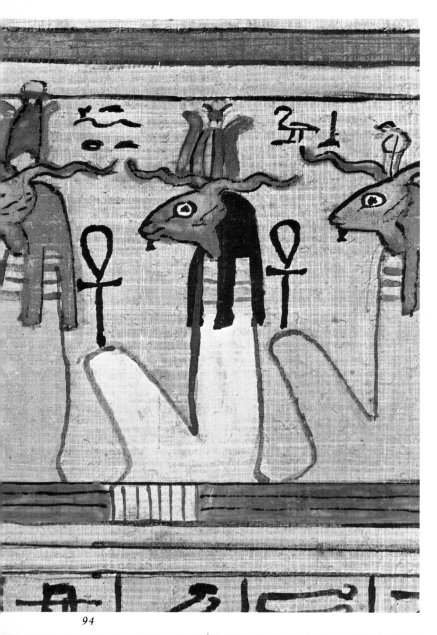

94

Plate 94

The ram was a ubiquitus creature in the mythology of ancient Egypt. The ram-headed Amon wielded a power no other god of the living could rival; there was also the creator god Khnum – a very old god indeed represented by a now extinct species like the one shown here. There was another ram-headed god in the Faiyum, Harsaphes, who became a state deity in the Seventh Dynasty and was associated with Osiris – he must have been a fertility god. Yet another was the ancient Ram of Mendes, who plays a part in the story of Horus and Set, and was represented by a real ram who enjoyed a cult like that of the Apis bulls. Other centres of ram worship were Hermopolis and Lycopolis, and Busiris which was believed to be the original centre of the cult of Osiris. The Ram of Mendes is seen in this papyrus of the Eighteenth Dynasty as the soul of Osiris, and wears the *atef* crown.

95

Plate 95

One of the traditions surrounding the coming of Ra told of the primordial hill at Heliopolis, upon which a temple was built to house an obelisk with gilded surfaces. This was the most sacred object in the city; the Benben stone which caught the rays of the rising sun. On this stone alighted a phoenix, the Bennu bird – Ra himself. The call of the Bennu bird heralded the news of creation. Ra is seen in two manifestations in this painting from the tomb of Sennutem; as Ra-Harakhte wearing the sun disk, and as the phoenix wearing the *atef* crown.

Plate 96

Aglazed figure of the Twenty-sixth Dynasty showing a sow and her piglets. Surprisingly, perhaps, mother sows were sacred to the sky goddess Nut; but she was also one of the mother goddesses of ancient Egypt so this is another aspect of fertility. She was sometimes portrayed as a sow with her piglets painted on her belly, and the tradition was that she swallowed them every morning – the mother goddess and sky goddess colliding there since the piglets were believed to be the stars which were extinguished in the sky when the sun shone.

11976

SOW AND PIGLETS

THE SOW WAS SACRED TO THE GODDESS OF THE SKY, N

Glazed composition.   Saite Period, c. 600 E

97

98
99

Plate 97

Cats were sacred to the people of the Delta from predynastic times and the most famous of the cat goddesses was Bast. Another known to us was Maldet, honoured during the First Dynasty. Cats were held in such honour, particularly in the days of the Ptolemies, that strangers in Egypt had to be very careful lest they harm them, however accidentally. Herodotus witnessed the murder of a Roman by an infuriated mob of Egyptians because he had accidentally killed a cat. The one shown here is from the papyrus of Hunefer, now in the British Museum. Bast, accompanying the solar barque through the regions of night, defeats the serpent Apep, the adversary of Ra.

Plate 98

A relief from Karnak depicting a vulture. The disposers of carrion are not molested in tropical countries and in Egypt it was inevitable that the steps from there to honour, and on to sanctification, would be short ones. Inevitable also would have been the vulture goddess's place as one of those concerned with death. Nekhebet, the vulture goddess, had a cult centre of her own on the right bank of the Nile at the city of Nekheb, and she remained the protective goddess of Upper Egypt throughout the country's long history.

Plate 99

The bull, the great symbol of strength and the generative power of the male, was the cult of more than one god in a Land where fruitfulness and renewal were of primary importance. The most famous was Apis but there were two others, Mnevis and Buchis. Mnevis was formally worshipped at Heliopolis but it is believed that a bull cult existed there in predynastic times. The life of Mnevis was said to repeat that of Osiris at each stage of the cycle. The cult centre of Buchis was at Hermonthis, close to Thebes, but he was a latecomer to Egypt, there is no mention of him before the Thirtieth Dynasty. The bull was also associated with the ithyphallic god Min, and in Ptolemaic times worship was accorded to the Golden bull of Canopus in the Delta. This relief from Medinet Habu, of the Nineteenth Dynasty, is another representation of Apis, with the sun disk and the *ankh*, the symbol of life.

Plate 100

A beautifully fashioned falcon from a mummy wrapping of the late Ptolemaic period. With its soaring flight the falcon was a natural choice as the representative of the god of the sky, and we have seen how readily the bird took its place in formalized religion. Some authorities believe that the cult began in Libya and that people from there were early conquerors of Egypt. The falcon turns up so often – he is connected with Ra, Horus and Seker to name only three gods – that it is probable that the bird had natural cults in many parts of Egypt and these came together over a period of time.

100

ACKNOWLEDGMENTS

The publishers would like to thank the following individuals and organizations for their kind permission to reproduce the pictures in this book: -

Plate Numbers

C M Dixon   21, 30, 56, 86, 89, 91, 93, 95, 96, 97.

Andre Held, Ziolo   68.

Michael Holford   5, 6, 7, 11, 17, 18, 19, 20, 22, 23, 26, 33, 36, 37, 38,
                   39, 42, 46, 47, 49, 51, 54, 63, 79, 83, 85, 88, 90, 92,
                   94, 98, 99, 100.

William Macquitty 8, 24, 29, 31, 45, 50, 64, 71, 74, 76, 77, 78, 80, 81,
                   82, 84.

Roger Wood Studio 1, 2, 3, 4, 9, 10, 12, 13, 14, 15, 16, 25, 27, 28, 32, 34,
                   35, 40, 41, 43, 44, 48, 52, 53, 55, 57, 58, 59, 62, 65,
                   66, 67, 69, 70, 72, 73, 75, 87.

Ziolo   60, 61.